CHARLES DICKENS

CHARLES DICKENS

CRESCENT BOOKS
NEW YORK • AVENEL

This edition published 1995 by Crescent Books,
distributed by Random House Value Publishing, Inc.
40 Engelhard Avenue, Avenel, New Jersey 07001.

Random House
New York • Toronto • London • Sydney • Auckland

First published 1993 by Aurum Press Ltd,
25 Bedford Avenue, London WC1B 3AT

A CIP catalog record for this book is available from the Library of Congress.

ISBN 0-517-14253-8

Printed and bound in China by Regent Publishing Services

10 9 8 7 6 5 4 3 2 1

We have to go back to Shakespeare to find a writer who, through fiction, has so enriched the thought of the people. Admit all Dickens's faults twice over, we still have one of the greatest writers of modern times.

JEROME K. JEROME

The name of the street catching Mr Dickens's eye, he suddenly exclaimed, "By Jove! here is the place where I was born", and acting on his suggestion, we walked up and down the terrace for some time, speculating as to which of the houses had the right to call itself his cradle. Beyond a recollection that there was a small front garden to the house he had no idea of the place – for he was only two years old when his father was removed to London from

Portsmouth. As the houses were nearly all alike, and each had a small front garden, we were not much helped in our quest by Mr Dickens's recollections, and great was the laughter at his humorous conjectures. He must have lived in one house because "it looked so like his father"; another one must have been his home because it looked like the birthplace of a man who had deserted it; a third was very like the cradle of a puny, weak youngster such as he had been; and so on, through the row . . . but as none of the houses in Landport Terrace [Dolby's mistake – it was Mile End Terrace] could cry out and say . . . "That boy was born here!" the mystery remained unsolved, and we passed on.

GEORGE DOLBY, DICKENS'S READING TOUR MANAGER

The blacking warehouse was the last house on the left-hand side of the way, at old Hungerford Stairs. It was a crazy, tumble-down old house, abutting of course on the river, and literally over-run with rats...

Until old Hungerford Market was pulled down, until old Hungerford Stairs were destroyed, and the very nature of the ground changed, I never had the courage to go back to the place where my servitude began. I never saw it. I could not go near it ... My old way home by the Borough made me cry, after my eldest child could speak.

CHARLES DICKENS, AUTOBIOGRAPHICAL FRAGMENT

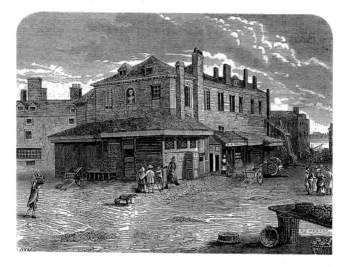

$\mathcal{T}$HE LAWYER'S CLERK

I was well acquainted with Dickens's parents, and, being then in practice in Gray's Inn, they asked me if I could find employment for him. He was a bright, clever-looking youth, and I took him as a clerk. He came to me in May 1827, and left in November 1828; and I have now an account-book which he used to keep of petty disbursements in the office, in which he charged himself with the modest salary first of thirteen shillings and sixpence, and afterwards of fifteen shillings a week. Several incidents took place in the office of which he must have been a keen observer, as I recognized some of them in his *Pickwick* and *Nickleby*; and I am much mistaken if some of his characters had not their originals in persons I well remember.

EDWARD BLACKMORE, SOLICITOR

THE YOUNG DICKENS

A look of youthfulness first attracted you, and then a candour and openness of expression which made you sure of the qualities within. The features were very good. He had a capital forehead, a firm nose with full wide nostrils, eyes wonderfully beaming with intellect and running over with humour and cheerfulness, and a rather prominent mouth strongly marked with sensibility. The head was altogether well-formed and symmetrical, and the air and carriage of it were extremely spirited. The hair so scant and grizzled in later days was then of a rich brown and most luxuriant abundance, and the bearded face of his last two decades had hardly a vestige of hair or whisker; but there was that in the face as I first recollect it which no time could change, and which remained implanted on it unalterably to the last. This was the quickness, keenness and practical power, the eager, restless, energetic outlook on each several feature, that seemed to tell so little of a student or writer of books, and so much of a man of action and business in the world. Light and motion flashed from every part of it. *It was as if made of steel*, was said of it, four or five years after the time to which I am referring, by a most original and delicate observer, the late Mrs Carlyle. "What a face is his to meet in a drawing-room!" wrote Leigh Hunt to me, the morning after I made them known to each other. "It has the life and soul in it of fifty human beings".

JOHN FORSTER, BIOGRAPHER

Dickens delivering his first manuscript.

9

NEWGATE PRISON

Leaving this room also by an opposite door, we found ourself in the lodge which opens on the Old Bailey, one side of which is plentifully garnished with a choice collection of heavy sets of irons, including those worn by the redoubtable Jack Sheppard – genuine; and those said to have been graced by the sturdy limbs of the no less celebrated Dick Turpin – doubtful. From this lodge a heavy oaken gate, bound with iron, studded with nails of the same material, and guarded by another turnkey, opens on a few steps, if we remember right, which terminate in a narrow and dismal stone passage, running parallel with the Old Bailey, and leading to the different yards, through a number of tortuous and intricate windings, guarded in their turn by huge gates and gratings, whose appearance is sufficient to dispel at once the slightest hope of escape that any newcomer may have entertained; and the very recollection of which, on eventually traversing the place again, involves one in a maze of confusion.

SKETCHES BY BOZ

$\mathcal{D}$ICKENS'S LONDON

He could imitate, in a manner that I have never heard equalled, the low population of the streets of London in all their varieties, and the popular singers of that day, whether comic or patriotic; as to his acting, he could give us Shakespeare by the ten minutes, and imitate all the leading actors of the time. He told me he had often taken part in amateur theatricals before he came to us. Having been in London for two years, I thought I knew something of the town, but after a little talk with Dickens I found that I knew nothing. He knew it all from Bow to Brentford.

GEORGE LEAR, FELLOW CLERK

"Oh you dear – " said Mrs Bardell.

Mr Pickwick started.

"Oh you kind, good, playful dear," said Mrs Bardell; and without more ado, she rose from her chair, and flung her arms round Mr Pickwick's neck, with a cataract of tears, and a chorus of sobs.

"Bless my soul," cried the astonished Mr Pickwick – "Mrs Bardell my good woman – dear me, what a situation – pray consider – Mrs Bardell, don't – if anybody should come – "

"Oh, let them come," exclaimed Mrs Bardell, frantically; "I'll never leave you – dear, kind, good soul;" and, with these words, Mrs Bardell clung the tighter.

"Mercy upon me," said Mr Pickwick, struggling violently; "I hear somebody coming up the stairs. Don't, don't, there's a good creature, don't." But entreaty and remonstrance were alike unavailing: for Mrs Bardell had fainted in Mr Pickwick's arms; and before he could gain time to deposit her on a chair, Master Bardell entered the room, ushering in Mr Tupman, Mr Winkle, and Mr Snodgrass.

Mr Pickwick was struck motionless and speechless. He stood with his lovely burden in his arms, gazing vacantly on the countenances of his friends, without the slightest attempt at recognition or explanation. They, in their turn, stared at him; and Master Bardell, in his turn, stared at everybody.

THE PICKWICK PAPERS

To ladies and gentlemen who are not in the habit of devoting themselves practically to the science of penmanship, writing a letter is no easy task; it being always considered necessary in such cases for the writer to recline his head on his left arm, so as to place his eyes as nearly as possible on a level with the paper, while glancing sideways at the letters he is constructing to form with his tongue imaginary characters to correspond. These motions, although unquestionably of the greatest assistance to original composition, retard in some degree the progress of the writer; and Sam had unconsciously been a full hour and a half writing words in small text, smearing out letters with his little finger, and putting in new ones which required going over very often to render them visible through the old blots, when he was roused by the opening of the door and the entrance of his parent.

"Vell, Sammy," said the father.

"Vell, my Prooshan Blue," responded the son, laying down his pen. "What's the last bulletin about mother-in-law?"

"Mrs Veller passed a very good night, but is uncommon perwerse, and unpleasant this mornin'. Signed upon oath, S Veller, Esquire, Senior. That's the last vun as was issued, Sammy," replied Mr Weller, untying his shawl.

"No better yet?" inquired Sam.

"All the symptoms aggerawated," replied Mr Weller, shaking his head. "But wot's that, you're a doin' of? Pursuit of knowledge under difficulties, Sammy?"

"I've done now," said Sam with slight embarrassment; "I've been a writin'."

"So I see," replied Mr Weller. "Not to any young 'ooman, I hope, Sammy?"

"Why it's no use a sayin' it ain't," replied Sam, "It's a walentine."

"A what!" exclaimed Mr Weller, apparently horror-stricken by the word.

"A walentine," replied Sam.

"Samivel, Samivel" said Mr Weller, in reproachful accents, "I didn't think you'd ha' done it. Arter the warnin' you've had o' your father's wicious propensities; arter all I've said to you upon this here wery subject; arter actiwally seein' and bein' in the company o' your own mother-in-law, vich I should ha' thought wos a moral lesson as no man could never ha' forgotten to his dyin' day! I didn't think you'd ha' done it, Sammy, I didn't think you'd ha' done it!" These reflections were too much for the good old man. He raised Sam's tumbler to his lips and drank off its contents.

THE PICKWICK PAPERS

Oliver Twist and his companions suffered the tortures of slow starvation for three months; at last they got so voracious and wild with hunger, that one boy, who was tall for his age, and hadn't been used to that sort of thing (for his father had kept a small cook-shop), hinted darkly to his companions, that unless he had another basin of gruel *per diem*, he was afraid he might some night happen to eat the boy who slept next him, who happened to be a weakly youth of tender age. He had a wild, hungry eye; and they implicitly believed him. A council was held; lots were cast who should walk up to the master after supper that evening, and ask for more; and it fell to Oliver Twist.

The evening arrived; the boys took their places. The master, in his cook's uniform, stationed himself at the copper; his pauper assistants ranged themselves behind him; the gruel was served out; and a long grace was said over the short commons. The gruel disappeared; the boys whispered to each other, and winked at Oliver; while his next neighbours nudged him. Child as he was, he was desperate with hunger, and reckless with misery. He rose from the table; and advancing to the master, basin and spoon in hand, said, somewhat alarmed at his own temerity:

"Please, Sir, I want some more."

The master was a fat, healthy man; but he turned very pale. He gazed in stupefied astonishment on the small rebel for some seconds, and then clung for support to the copper. The assistants were paralysed with wonder; the boys with fear.

"What!" said the master at length, in a faint voice.

"Please, Sir," replied Oliver, "I want some more."

The master was a fat, healthy man; but he turned very pale. He gazed in stupefied astonishment on the small rebel for some sec-

onds, and then clung for support to the copper. The assistants were paralysed with wonder; the boys with fear.

"What!" said the master at length, in a faint voice.

"Please, Sir," replied Oliver, "I want some more."

The master aimed a blow at Oliver's head with the ladle; pinioned him in his arms; and shrieked aloud for the beadle.

The board were sitting in solemn conclave, when Mr Bumble rushed into the room in great excitement, and addressing the gentleman in the high chair, said,

"Mr Limbkins, I beg your pardon, Sir! Oliver Twist has asked for more!"

OLIVER TWIST

"You see he knows me!" cried Nancy, appealing to the bystanders. "He can't help himself. Make him come home, there's good people, or he'll kill his dear mother and father, and break my heart!"

"What the devil's this ?" said a man, bursting out of a beer-shop, with a white dog at his heels; "young Oliver! Come home to your poor mother, you young dog! Come home directly."

"I don't belong to them. I don't know them. Help! help!" cried Oliver, struggling in the man's powerful grasp.

"Help!" repeated the man. "Yes; I'll help you, you young rascal! What books are these? You've been a stealing 'em, have you? Give 'em here." With these words, the man tore the volumes from his grasp, and struck him on the head.

"That's right!" cried a looker-on, from a garret-window. "That's the only way of bringing him to his senses!"

"To be sure!" cried a sleepy-faced carpenter, casting an approving look at the garret-window.

"It'll do him good!" said the two women.

"And he shall have it, too!" rejoined the man, administering another blow, and seizing Oliver by the collar. "Come on, you young villain! Here, Bull's-eye, mind him boy! Mind him!"

Weak with recent illness; stupefied by the blows and the suddenness of the attack; terrified by the fierce growling of the dog, and the brutality of the man; and overpowered by the conviction of the bystanders that he really was the hardened little wretch he was described to be; what could one poor child do! Darkness

had set in; it was a low neighbourhood; no help was near; resistance was useless. In another moment, he was dragged into a labyrinth of dark narrow courts, and forced along them, at a pace which rendered the few cries he dared to give utterance to, wholly unintelligible. It was of little moment, indeed, whether they were intelligible or no; for there was nobody to care for them, had they been ever so plain.

OLIVER TWIST

DICKENS AND THE POOR

On the Fifth of last November, I, the Conductor of this Journal, accompanied by a friend well known to the public, accidentally strayed into Whitechapel. It was a miserable evening; very dark, very muddy, and raining hard.

There are many woeful sights in that part of London, and it has been well known to me in most of its aspects for many years. We had forgotten the mud and rain in slowly walking along and looking about us, when we found ourselves, at eight o'clock, before the Workhouse.

Crouched against the wall of the Workhouse, in the dark street, on the muddy pavement stones, with the rain raining upon them, were five bundles of rags. They were motionless, and had no resemblance to the human form. Five great beehives, covered with rags – five dead bodies taken out of graves, tied neck and heels, and covered with rags – would have looked like those five bundles upon which the rain rained down in the public street.

"What is this!" said my companion. "What is this!"

"Some miserable people shut out of the Casual Ward, I think," said I.

We had stopped before the five ragged mounds and were quite rooted to the spot by their horrible appearance. Five awful Sphinxes by the wayside, crying to every passer-by, "Stop and guess! What is to be the end of a state of society that leaves us here!"

As we stood looking at them, a decent working-man, having the appearance of a stone-mason, touched me on the shoulder.

"This is an awful sight, sir," said he, "in a Christian country!"

MEMORIES AND SKETCHES

I feel in my heart the love which Dickens felt for the poor and the disinherited, for troubled childhoods, and all the miseries of life in big cities. Like him, my first steps in life were heart-rendingly unhappy; like him, I was forced to earn my bread before I was sixteen years of age, and in this I imagine lies our greatest resemblance.

ALPHONSE DAUDET

He is a very great loss. He had a large loving mind and the strongest sympathy for the poorer classes.

QUEEN VICTORIA'S JOURNAL, 11 JUNE 1870, ON THE DEATH OF DICKENS

KATE NICKLEBY

Quite unconscious of the demonstrations of their amorous neighbour, or their effects upon the susceptible bosom of her mama, Kate Nickleby had, by this time, begun to enjoy a settled feeling of tranquillity and happiness, to which, even in occasional and transitory glimpses, she had long been a stranger. Living under the same roof with the beloved brother from whom she had been so suddenly and hardly separated; with a mind at ease, and free from any persecutions which could call a blush into her cheek, or a pang into her heart, she seemed to have passed into a new state of being. Her former cheerfulness was restored, her step regained its elasticity and lightness, the colour which had forsaken her cheek visited it once again, and Kate Nickleby looked more beautiful than ever.

NICHOLAS NICKLEBY

What a host of beauties crowd on our grateful recollection... With what pleasant thoughts it has stocked our memory, with what true and tender sentiments enriched our hearts, with what healthy and manly morals instructed our minds. With how much vivid distinctness each character takes its place before us, how plainly we see the individualities of each, the form of their faces, the accident of their habits, the nicer peculiarity of their minds. These are triumphs which only belong to a first-rate writer.

JOHN FORSTER

"Look at him!" said Varden, divided between admiration of the bird and a kind of fear of him. "Was there ever such a knowing imp as that! Oh he's a dreadful fellow!"

The raven, with his head very much on one side, and his bright eye shining like a diamond, preserved a thoughtful silence for a few seconds, and then replied in a voice so hoarse and distant, that it seemed to come through his thick feathers rather than out of his mouth.

"Halloa, halloa, halloa! What's the matter here! Keep up your spirits. Never say die. Bow wow wow. I'm a devil, I'm a devil, I'm a devil. Hurrah!" – And then, as if exulting in his infernal character, he began to whistle.

"I more than half believe he speaks the truth. Upon my word I do," said Varden. "Do you see how he looks at me, as if he knew what I was saying?"

To which the bird, balancing himself on tiptoe, as it were, and moving his body up and down in a sort of grave dance, rejoined, "I'm a devil, I'm a devil, I'm a devil," and flapped his wings against his sides as if he were bursting with laughter. Barnaby clapped his hands, and fairly rolled upon the ground in an ecstasy of delight.

"Strange companions, Sir," said the locksmith, shaking his head and looking from one to the other. "The bird has all the wit."

BARNABY RUDGE

I t was a little old man with long grey hair, whose face and figure as he held the light above his head and looked before him as he approached, I could plainly see. Though much altered by age, I fancied I could recognize in his spare and slender form something of that delicate mould which I had noticed in the child. Their bright blue eyes were certainly alike, but his face was so deeply furrowed and so very full of care, that here all resemblance ceased.

The place through which he made his way at leisure was one of those receptacles for old and curious things which seem to crouch in odd corners of this town and to hide their musty treasures from the public eye in jealousy and distrust. There were suits of mail standing like ghosts in armour here and there, fantastic carvings brought from monkish cloisters, rusty weapons of various kinds, distorted figures in china and wood and iron and ivory, tapestry and strange furniture that might have been designed in dreams. The haggard aspect of the little old man was wonderfully suited to the place; he might have groped among old churches and tombs and deserted houses and gathered all the spoils with his own hands. There was nothing in the whole collection but was in keeping with himself; nothing that looked older or more worn than he.

THE OLD CURIOSITY SHOP

LITTLE NELL

She left the chapel – very slowly and often turning back to gaze again – and coming to a low door, which plainly led into the tower, opened it, and climbed the winding stair in darkness; save where she looked down through narrow loopholes on the place she had left, or caught a glimmering vision of the dusty bells. At length she gained the end of the ascent and stood upon the turret top.

Oh! the glory of the sudden burst of light; the freshness of the fields and woods, stretching away on every side and meeting the bright blue sky; the cattle grazing in the pasturage; the smoke, that, coming from among the trees, seemed to rise upward from the green earth; the children yet at their gambols down below – all, everything, so beautiful and happy! It was like passing from death to life; it was drawing nearer Heaven.

The children were gone by the time she emerged into the porch, and locked the door. As she passed the school-house she could hear the busy hum of voices. Her friend had begun his labours only that day. The noise grew louder, and, looking back, she saw the boys come trooping out and disperse themselves with merry shouts and play.

"It's a good thing," thought the child, "I am very glad they pass the church." And then she stopped, to fancy how the noise would sound inside, and how gently it would seem to die away upon the ear.

THE OLD CURIOSITY SHOP

His hours and days were spent by rule. He rose at a certain time, he retired at another, and, though no precisian, it was not often that arrangements varied. His hours for writing were between breakfast and luncheon, and when there was any work to be done, no temptation was sufficiently strong to cause it to be neglected. The order and regularity followed him through the day. His mind was essentially methodical, and in his long walks, in his recreations, in his labour, he was governed by rules laid down for himself – rules well studied beforehand, and rarely departed from.

ANONYMOUS FRIEND

He was usually alone when at work, though there were, of course, some occasional exceptions, and I myself constituted such an exception. During our life at Tavistock House I had a long and serious illness, with an almost equally long convalescence. During the latter my father suggested that I should be carried every day into his study, to remain with him, and, although I was fearful of disturbing him, he assured me that he desired to have me with him. On one of these mornings I was lying on the sofa endeavouring to keep perfectly quiet, while my father wrote busily and rapidly at his desk; when he suddenly jumped from his chair and rushed to a mirror which hung near, and in which I could see the reflection of some extraordinary facial contortions which he was making. He returned rapidly to his desk, wrote furiously for a few minutes, and then went to the mirror. The facial pantomime was resumed, and then turning inwards, but evidently not seeing me, he began talking rapidly in a low voice. Ceasing this soon, however, he returned once more to his desk, where he remained silently writing until luncheon-time. It was a curious experience for me, and one of which I did not until later years fully appreciate the purport. Then I knew that with his natural intensity he had thrown himself completely into the character that he was creating, and that for the time being he had not only lost sight of his surroundings, but had actually become in action, as in imagination, the personality of his pen.

MAMIE DICKENS, DAUGHTER

The cellar-door flew open with a booming sound, and then he heard the noise much louder, on the floors below; then coming up the stairs; then coming straight towards his door.

"It's humbug still!" said Scrooge. "I won't believe it."

His colour changed though, when, without a pause, it came on through the heavy door, and passed into the room before his eyes. Upon its coming in, the dying flame leaped up, as though it cried "I know him! Marley's Ghost!" and fell again.

The same face: the very same. Marley in his pigtail, usual waistcoat, tights and boots; the tassels on the latter bristling, like his pigtail, and his coat-skirts, and the hair upon his head. The chain he drew was clasped about his middle. It was long, and wound about him like a tail; and it was made (for Scrooge observed it closely) of cashboxes, keys, padlocks, ledgers, deeds, and heavy purses wrought in steel. His body was transparent; so that Scrooge, observing him, and looking through his waistcoat, could see the two buttons on his coat behind.

Scrooge had often heard it said that Marley had no bowels, but he had never believed it until now.

No, nor did he believe it even now. Though he looked the phantom through and through, and saw it standing before him; though he felt the chilling influence of its death-cold eyes; and marked the very texture of the folded kerchief bound about its head and chin, which wrapper he had not observed before: he was still incredulous, and fought against his senses.

"How now!" said Scrooge, caustic and cold as ever. "What do you want with me?"

"Much!" – Marley's voice, no doubt about it.

A Christmas Carol

BOB CRATCHIT AND TINY TIM

"What has ever got your precious father then?" said Mrs Cratchit. "And your brother, Tiny Tim! And Martha warn't as late last Christmas Day by half-an-hour!"

"Here's Martha, mother!" said a girl, appearing as she spoke.

"Here's Martha, mother!" cried the two young Cratchits. "Hurrah! There's *such* a goose, Martha!"

"Why, bless your heart alive, my dear, how late you are!" said Mrs Cratchit, kissing her a dozen times, and taking off her shawl and bonnet for her with officious zeal.

"We'd a deal of work to finish up last night," replied the girl, "and had to clear away this morning, mother!"

"Well! Never mind so long as you are come," said Mrs Cratchit. "Sit ye down before the fire, my dear, and have a warm, Lord bless ye!"

"No, no! There's father coming," cried the two young Cratchits, who were everywhere at once. "Hide, Martha, hide!"

So Martha hid herself, and in came little Bob, the father, with at least three feet of comforter exclusive of the fringe, hanging down before him; and his threadbare clothes darned up and brushed, to look seasonable; and Tiny Tim upon his shoulder. Alas for Tiny Tim, he bore a little crutch, and had his limbs supported by an iron frame!

A CHRISTMAS CAROL

Who can listen to objection regarding such a book as this? The last two people I heard speak of it were women; neither knew the other or the author, and both said by way of criticism, "God bless him!" What a feeling is this for a writer to be able to inspire, and what a reward to reap!

W. M. THACKERAY

"Bless my life, Miss Pecksniffs!" cried Mrs Todgers, aloud, "your dear pa's took very poorly!"

Mr Pecksniff straightened himself by a surprising effort, as every one turned hastily towards him; and standing on his feet, regarded the assembly with a look of ineffable wisdom. Gradually it gave place to a smile; a feeble, helpless, melancholy smile; bland, almost to sickliness. "Do not repine, my friends," said Mr Pecksniff, tenderly. "Do not weep for me. It is chronic." And with these words, after making a futile attempt to pull off his shoes, he fell into the fire-place.

The youngest gentleman in the company had him out in a second. Yes, before a hair upon his head was singed, he had him on the hearth-rug. – Her father!

She was almost beside herself. So was her sister. Jinkins consoled them both. They all consoled them. Everybody had something to say except the youngest gentleman in the company, who with a noble self-devotion did the heavy work, and held up Mr Pecksniff's head without being taken any notice of by anybody. At last they gathered round, and agreed to carry him up-stairs to bed. The youngest gentleman in the company was rebuked by Jinkins for tearing Mr Pecksniff's coat! Ha, ha! But no matter.

They carried him up-stairs, and crushed the youngest gentleman at every step. His bedroom was at the top of the house, and it was a long way; but they got him there in course of time. He asked them frequently upon the road for a little drop of something to drink. It seemed an idiosyncrasy. The youngest gentleman in the company proposed a draught of water. Mr Pecksniff called him opprobrious names for the suggestion.

MARTIN CHUZZLEWIT

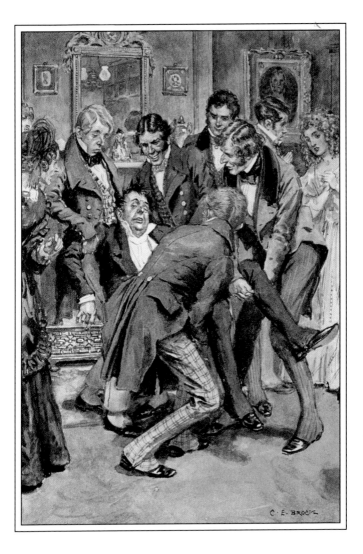

Sarah Gamp

She was a fat old woman, this Mrs Gamp, with a husky voice and a moist eye, which she had a remarkable power of turning up, and only showing the white of. Having very little neck, it cost her some trouble to look over herself, if one may say so, at those to whom she talked. She wore a very rusty black gown, rather the worse for snuff, and a shawl and bonnet to correspond. In these dilapidated articles of dress she had, on principle, arrayed herself, time out of mind, on such occasions as the present; for this at once expressed a decent amount of veneration for the deceased, and invited the next of kin to present her with a fresher suit of weeds: an appeal so frequently successful, that the very fetch and ghost of Mrs Gamp, bonnet and all, might be seen hanging up, any hour in the day, in at least a dozen of the second-hand clothes shops about Holborn. The face of Mrs Gamp – the nose in particular – was somewhat red and swollen, and it was difficult to enjoy her society without becoming conscious of a smell of spirits. Like most persons who have attained to great eminence in their profession, she took to hers very kindly; insomuch, that setting aside her natural predilections as a woman, she went to a lying-in or a laying-out with equal zest and relish.

Martin Chuzzlewit

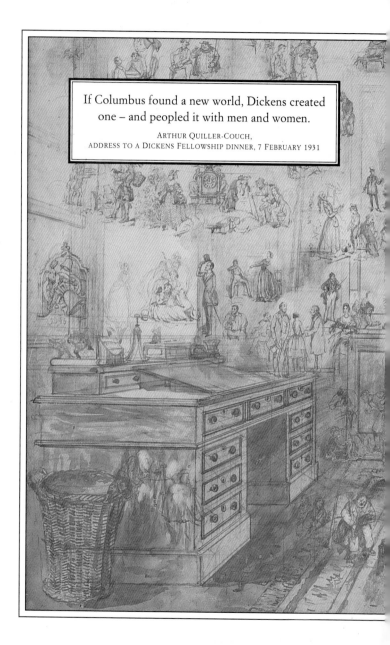

If Columbus found a new world, Dickens created
one – and peopled it with men and women.

ARTHUR QUILLER-COUCH,
ADDRESS TO A DICKENS FELLOWSHIP DINNER, 7 FEBRUARY 1931

THE SPIRITS OF THE BELLS

He saw the tower, whither his charmed footsteps had brought him, swarming with dwarf phantoms, spirits, elfin creatures of the Bells. He saw them leaping, flying, dropping, pouring from the Bells without a pause. He saw them, round him on the ground; above him, in the air; clambering from him, by the ropes below; looking down upon him, from the massive iron-girded beams; peeping in upon him, through the chinks and loopholes in the walls; spreading away and away from him in enlarging circles, as the water-ripples give place to a huge stone that suddenly comes splashing in among them. He saw them, of all aspects and all shapes. He saw them ugly, handsome, crippled, exquisitely formed. He saw them young, he saw them old, he saw them kind, he saw them cruel, he saw them merry, he saw them grim; he saw them dance, and heard them sing; he saw them tear their hair, and heard them howl. He saw the air thick with them. He saw them come and go, incessantly. He saw them riding downward, soaring upward, sailing off afar, perching near at hand, all restless and all violently active. Stone, and brick, and slate, and tile, became transparent to him as to them. He saw them *in* the houses, busy at the sleepers' beds. He saw them soothing people in their dreams; he saw them beating them with knotted whips; he saw them yelling in their ears; he saw them playing softest music on their pillows; he saw them cheering some with the songs of birds and the perfume of flowers; he saw them flashing awful faces on the troubled rest of others, from enchanted mirrors which they carried in their hands.

THE CHIMES

*I*N THE *C*APTAIN'S *P*ARLOUR

"*D*o you live here?" asked Florence.

"Yes, my lady lass," returned the Captain.

"Oh Captain Cuttle!" cried Florence, putting her hands together, and speaking wildly. "Save me! Keep me here! Let no one know where I am! I'll tell you what has happened by-and-by, when I can. I have no one in the world to go to. Do not send me away!"

"Send you away, my lady lass!" exclaimed the Captain. "*You*, my Heart's Delight! Stay a bit! We'll put up this here dead-light, and take a double turn on the key!"

With these words, the Captain, using his one hand and his hook with the greatest dexterity, got out the shutter of the door, put it up, made it all fast, and locked the door itself.

When he came back to the side of Florence, she took his hand and kissed it. The helplessness of the action, the appeal it made to him, the confidence it expressed, the unspeakable sorrow in her face, the pain of mind she had too plainly suffered, and was suffering then, his knowledge of her past history, her present lonely, worn, and unprotected appearance, all so rushed upon the good Captain together, that he fairly overflowed with compassion and gentleness...

Nothing would induce the Captain to believe that it was possible for Florence to walk up-stairs. If he could have got the idea into his head, he would have considered it an outrageous breach of hospitality to allow her to do so. Florence was too weak to dispute the point, and the Captain carried her up out of hand, laid her down, and covered her with a great watch-coat.

DOMBEY AND SON

MR MICAWBER

The counting-house clock was at half-past twelve, and there was general preparation for going to dinner, when Mr Quinion tapped at the counting-house window, and beckoned to me to go in. I went in, and found there a stoutish, middle-aged person, in a brown surtout and black tights and shoes, with no more hair upon his head (which was a large one, and very shining) than there is upon an egg, and with a very extensive face, which he turned full upon me. His clothes were shabby, but he had an imposing shirt-collar on. He carried a jaunty sort of a stick, with a large pair of rusty tassels to it; and a quizzing-glass hung outside his coat – for ornament, I afterwards found, as he very seldom looked through it, and couldn't see anything when he did.

"This," said Mr Quinion, in allusion to myself, "is he."

"This," said the stranger, with a certain condescending roll in his voice, and a certain indescribable air of doing something genteel, which impressed me very much, "is Master Copperfield. I hope I see you well, Sir ?"

I said I was very well, and hoped he was. I was sufficiently ill at ease, Heaven knows; but it was not in my nature to complain much at that time of my life, so I said I was very well, and hoped he was.

"I am," said the stranger, "thank Heaven, quite well. I have received a letter from Mr Murdstone, in which he mentions that he would desire me to receive into an apartment in the rear of my house, which is at present unoccupied – and is, in short, to be let as a – in short," said the stranger, with a smile and in a burst of confidence, "as a bedroom – the young beginner whom I have now the pleasure to – " and the stranger waved his hand, and settled his chin in his shirt-collar.

"This is Mr Micawber," said Mr Quinion to me.

DAVID COPPERFIELD

$\mathcal{B}$ETSY TROTWOOD

M y aunt was a tall, hard-featured lady, but by no means ill-looking. There was an inflexibility in her face, in her voice, in her gait and carriage, amply sufficient to account for the effect she had made upon a gentle creature like my mother, but her features were rather handsome than otherwise, though unbending and austere. I particularly noticed that she had a very quick, bright eye. Her hair, which was grey, was arranged in two plain divisions, under what I believe would be called a mob-cap: I mean a cap, much more common then than now, with side-pieces fastening under the chin. Her dress was of a lavender colour, and perfectly neat; but scantily made, as if she desired to be as little encumbered as possible. I remember that I thought it, in form, more like a riding-habit with the superfluous skirt cut off, than anything else. She wore at her side a gentleman's gold watch, if I might judge from its size and make, with an appropriate chain and seals; she had some linen at her throat not unlike a shirt-collar, and things at her wrists like little shirt-wristbands.

DAVID COPPERFIELD

———◆———

In *David Copperfield*…characters swarm and life flows through into every cheek and cranny, some common feeling – youth, gaiety, hope – envelops the tumult, brings the scattered parts together, and invests the most perfect of all the Dickens novels with an atmosphere of beauty.

VIRGINIA WOOLF

LONDON FOG

Fog everywhere. Fog up the river, where it flows among green aits and meadows; fog down the river, where it rolls defiled among the tiers of shipping, and the waterside pollutions of a great (and dirty) city. Fog on the Essex marshes, fog on the Kentish heights. Fog creeping into the cabooses of collier-brigs; fog lying out on the yards, and hovering in the rigging of great ships; fog drooping on the gunwales of barges and small boats. Fog in the eyes and throats of ancient Greenwich pensioners, wheezing by the firesides of their wards; fog in the stem and bowl of the afternoon pipe of the wrathful skipper, down in his close cabin; fog cruelly pinching the toes and fingers of his shivering little 'prentice boy on deck. Chance people on the bridges peeping over the parapets into a nether sky of fog, with fog all round them, as if they were up in a balloon, and hanging in the misty clouds.

Gas looming through the fog in divers places in the streets, much as the sun may, from the spongey fields, be seen to loom by husbandman and ploughboy. Most of the shops lighted two hours before their time – as the gas seems to know, for it has a haggard and unwilling look.

The raw afternoon is rawest, and the dense fog is densest, and the muddy streets are muddiest, near that leaden-headed old obstruction, appropriate ornament for the threshold of a leaden-headed old corporation: Temple Bar. And hard by Temple Bar, in Lincoln's Inn Hall, at the very heart of the fog, sits the Lord High Chancellor in this High Court of Chancery.

Never can there come fog too thick, never can there come mud and mire too deep, to assort with the groping and floundering condition which this High Court of Chancery, most pestilent of hoary sinners, holds, this day, in the sight of heaven and earth.

On such an afternoon, if ever, the Lord Chancellor ought to be sitting here – as here he is – with a foggy glory round his head, softly fenced in with crimson cloth and curtains, addressed by a large advocate with great whiskers, a little voice, and an interminable brief, and outwardly directing his contemplation to the lantern in the roof, where he can see nothing but fog. On such an afternoon, some score members of the High Court of Chancery bar ought to be – as here they are – mistily engaged in one of the ten thousand stages of an endless cause, tripping one another up on slippery precedents, groping knee-deep in technicalities, running their goat-hair and horse-hair warded heads against walls of words, and making a pretence of equity with serious faces, as players might. On such an afternoon, the various solicitors in the cause, some two or three of whom have inherited it from their fathers, who made a fortune by it, ought to be – as are they not? – ranged in a line, in a long matted well (but you might look in vain for Truth at the bottom of it), between the registrar's red table and the silk gowns, with bills, cross-bills, answers, rejoinders, injunctions, affidavits, issues, references to masters, masters' reports, mountains of costly nonsense, piled before them. Well may the court be dim, with wasting candles here and there; well may the fog hang heavy in it, as if it would never get out.

BLEAK HOUSE

GAD'S HILL PLACE

Down at Gad's Hill, near Rochester, in Kent – Shakespeare's Gads Hill where Falstaff engaged in the robbery – is a quaint little country house of Queen Ann's time. I happened to be walking past, a year and a half or so ago with my sub-editor of *Household Words*, when I said to him: "You see that house? It has always a curious interest for me, because when I was a small boy down in these parts I thought it the most beautiful house (I suppose because of its famous old cedar trees) ever seen. And my poor father used to bring me to look at it, and used to say that if ever I grew up to be a clever man perhaps I might own that house, or another such house. In remembrance of which, I have always, in passing, looked to see if it was to be sold or let, and it has never been to me like any other house, and it has never changed at all." We came back to town and my friend went out to dinner. Next morning he came in great excitement, and said: "It is written `that you were to have that house at Gad's Hill Place. The lady I had allotted to me to take down to dinner yesterday began to speak of that neighbourhood, 'You know it?' I said. 'I have been there today.' 'Oh yes,' she said. 'I know it very well, I was a child there, in the house they call Gad's Hill Place. My father was the rector, and lived there many years. He has just died, has left it to me, and I want to sell it.'" "So," says the sub-editor, "you must buy it. Now or never!" I did, and hope to pass next summer there, though I may, perhaps, let it afterwards furnished from time to time.

CHARLES DICKENS, LETTER TO M. DE CERJAT

Along the Paris streets, the death-carts rumble, hollow and harsh. Six tumbrils carry the day's wine to La Guillotine. All the devouring and insatiate Monsters imagined since imagination could record itself, are fused in the one realization, Guillotine...

As the sombre wheels of the six carts go round, they seem to plough up a long crooked furrow among the populace in the streets. Ridges of faces are thrown to this side and to that, and the ploughs go steadily onwards. So used are the regular inhabitants of the houses to the spectacle, that in many windows there are no people, and in some the occupation of the hands is not so much as suspended, while the eyes survey the faces in the tumbrils. Here and there, the inmate has visitors to see the sight; then he points his finger, with something of the complacency of a curator or authorized exponent, to this cart and to this, and seems to tell who sat here yesterday, and who there the day before.

Of the riders in the tumbrils, some observe these things, and all things on their last roadside, with an impassive stare; others, with a lingering interest in the ways of life and men. Some, seated with drooping heads, are sunk in silent despair; again, there are some so heedful of their looks that they cast upon the multitude such glances as they have seen in theatres, and in pictures. Several close their eyes, and think, or try to get their straying thoughts together. Only one, and he a miserable creature, of a crazed aspect, is so shattered and made drunk by horror, that he sings, and tries to dance. Not one of the whole number appeals by look or gesture, to the pity of the people.

There is a guard of sundry horsemen riding abreast of the tumbrils, and faces are often turned up to some of them, and they are asked some question. It would seem to be always the same ques-

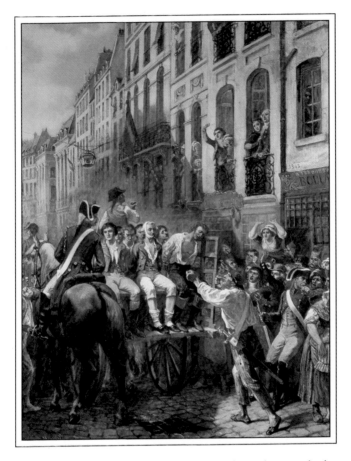

tion, for it is always followed by a press of people towards the third cart. The horsemen abreast of that cart, frequently point out one man in it with their swords. The leading curiosity is, to know which is he.

A TALE OF TWO CITIES

"I see a beautiful city and a brilliant people rising from this abyss, and, in their struggles to be truly free, in their triumphs and defeats, through long long years to come, I see the evil of this time and of the previous time of which this is the natural birth, gradually making expiation for itself and wearing out.

"I see the lives for which I lay down my life, peaceful, useful, prosperous and happy, in that England which I shall see no more. I see Her with a child upon her bosom, who bears my name...

"It is a far, far better thing that I do, than I have ever done; it is a far, far better rest that I go to than I have ever known."

A TALE OF TWO CITIES

Boston, Tuesday 7 April 1868

I not only read last Friday, when I was doubtful of being able to do so, but read as I never did before, and astonished the audience quite as much as myself. You never saw or heard such a scene of excitement.

DICKENS, LETTER TO HIS DAUGHTER

My father's name being Pirrip, and my Christian name Philip, my infant tongue could make of both names nothing longer or more explicit than Pip. So, I called myself Pip, and came to be called Pip.

I give Pirrip as my father's family name, on the authority of his tombstone and my sister – Mrs Joe Gargery, who married the blacksmith. As I never saw my father, or my mother, and never saw any likeness of either of them (for their days were long before the days of photographs), my first fancies regarding what they were like, were unreasonably derived from their tombstones. The shape of the letters on my father's gave me an odd idea that he was a square, stout, dark man, with curly black hair. From the character and turn of the inscription, "*Also Georgiana Wife of the Above,*" I drew a childish conclusion that my mother was freckled and sickly. To five little stone lozenges, each about a foot and a half long, which were arranged in a neat row beside their grave, and were sacred to the memory of five little brothers of mine – who gave up trying to get a living exceedingly early in that universal struggle – I am indebted for a belief I religiously entertained that they had all been born on their backs with their hands in their trousers-pockets, and had never taken them out in this state of existence.

Ours was the marsh country, down by the river, within, as the river wound, twenty miles of the sea. My first most vivid and broad impression of the identity of things, seems to me to have been gained on a memorable raw afternoon towards evening. At such a time I found out for certain, that this bleak place overgrown with nettles was the churchyard; and that Philip Pirrip, late of this parish, and also Georgiana wife of the above, were dead and buried; and that Alexander, Bartholomew, Abraham, Tobias, and Roger, infant children of the aforesaid, were also dead and buried; and that the dark flat wilderness beyond the churchyard, intersected with dykes and mounds and gates, with scattered cattle feeding on it, was the marshes; and that the low leaden line beyond was the river; and that the distant savage lair from which the wind was rushing, was the sea; and that the small bundle of shivers growing afraid of it all and beginning to cry, was Pip.

"Hold your noise!" cried a terrible voice, as a man started up from among the graves at the side of the church porch. "Keep still, you little devil, or I'll cut your throat!"

A fearful man, all in coarse grey, with a great iron on his leg. A man with no hat, and with broken shoes, and with an old rag tied round his head. A man who had been soaked in water and smothered in mud, and lamed by stones, and cut by flints, and stung by nettles, and torn by briars; who limped, and shivered, and glared and growled; and whose teeth chattered in his head as he seized me by the chin.

"O! Don't cut my throat sir," I pleaded in terror. "Pray don't do it, sir."

"Tell us your name!" said the man. "Quick!"

"Pip, sir."

"Once more," said the man, staring at me. "Give it mouth!"

"Pip. Pip, sir."

"Show us where you live," said the man. "Pint out the place!"

I pointed to where our village lay, on the flat in-shore among the alder trees and pollards, a mile or more from the church.

The man, after looking at me for a moment, turned me upside down, and emptied my pockets. There was nothing in them but a piece of bread.

GREAT EXPECTATIONS

THE OPIUM DEN

Shaking from head to foot, the man whose scattered conscious-
ness has thus fantastically pieced itself together, at length
rises, supports his trembling frame upon his arms, and looks
around. He is in the meanest and closest of small rooms.
Through the ragged window-curtain, the light of early day steals
in from a miserable court. He lies, dressed, across a large
unseemly bed, upon a bedstead that has indeed given way under
the weight upon it. Lying, also dressed and also across the bed,
not longwise, are a Chinaman, a Lascar, and a haggard woman.
The two first are in a sleep of stupor; the last is blowing at a kind
of pipe, to kindle it. And as she blows, and shading it with her
lean hand, concentrates its red spark of light, it serves in the dim
morning as a lamp to show him what he sees of her.

"Another?" says this woman, in a querulous, rattling whisper.
"Have another?"

He looks about him, with his hand to his forehead.

"Ye've smoked as many as five since ye come in at midnight,"
the woman goes on, as she chronically complains. "Poor me,
poor me, my head is so bad. Them two come in after ye. Ah, poor
me, the business is slack, is slack! Few Chinamen about the
Docks, and fewer Lascars, and no ships coming in, these say!
Here's another ready for ye, deary."

THE MYSTERY OF EDWIN DROOD

$\mathcal{T}$HE GENIUS OF DICKENS

It always seemed to me that no man ever devoted himself so entirely as Charles Dickens to things which he understood, and in which he could work with effect. Of other matters he seemed to have a disregard – and for many things almost a contempt which was marvellous. To literature in all its branches his attachment was deep – and his belief in it was a thorough conviction. He could speak about it as no other man spoke. He was always enthusiastic in its interests, ready to push on beginners, quick to encourage those who were winning their way to success, sympathetic with his contemporaries, and greatly generous to aid those who were failing. He thoroughly believed in literature, but in politics he seemed to have no belief at all. As years roll on we shall learn to appreciate his loss.

ANTHONY TROLLOPE

The good, the gentle, the high-gifted, ever-friendly, noble Dickens – every inch of him an Honest Man.

THOMAS CARLYLE

Think of all we owe Mr Dickens since those half-dozen years, the store of happy hours that he has made us pass, the kindly and pleasant companions whom he has introduced to us; the harmless laughter, the generous wit, the frank, manly, human love which he has taught us to feel! Every month of those years has brought us some kind token from this delightful genius. His books may have lost in art, perhaps, but could we afford to wait?

W. M. THACKERAY

$\mathcal{P}$ICTURE ACKNOWLEDGEMENTS

Bridgeman Art Library: 2, 5 & 15 (Dickens House Museum),
10 (Royal Holloway & Bedford New College), 11 (Royal
Academy, London), 13 and back jacket, 20 (Forbes Magazine
Collection), 23 (Fine Art Society, London), 24 & 45 (Victoria &
Albert Museum), 27 (Guildhall Library, Corporation of
London), 28 (Bradford Art Galleries & Museums),
55 (Giraudon/Galerie Dijol).
Dickens House Museum: 9, 31, 40–41, 53, 63.
Mary Evans Picture Library: 6, 7, 8, 18, 19, 25, 26, 30 and
back jacket, 38, 39, 48, 56.
Mansell Collection: 61.
Private collection: all others.